THE
TOXIC
BOSS
SURVIVAL
GUIDE

THE TOXIC BOSS SURVIVAL GUIDE

TACTICS FOR NAVIGATING THE WILDERNESS AT WORK

Craig Chappelow | Peter Ronayne | Bill Adams

Center for Creative Leadership

LEAD CONTRIBUTORS
Craig Chappelow, Peter Ronayne, Bill Adams

CONTRIBUTORS
Reggie Bennett, Mike Figliuolo, Donnie Horner, Harold
Scharlatt, Stevie Toepke

DIRECTOR, PEOPLE, PROCESS, PRODUCTS
Davida Sharpe

MANAGER, PUBLICATION DEVELOPMENT
Peter Scisco

EDITOR
Shaun Martin

DESIGN AND ILLUSTRATIONS
Diana Coe

RIGHTS AND PERMISSIONS
Kelly Lombardino

EDITORIAL BOARD
David Altman, Elaine Biech, Regina Eckert, Joan Gurvis,
Jennifer Habig, Kevin Liu, Neal Maillet, Jennifer Martineau,
Portia Mount, Laura Santana

CCL No. 001007
978-1-60491-769-7 – Print
978-1-60491-764-2 – Ebook

Cataloging in publication data on file with the Library of
Congress.

CONTENTS

AUTHORS' NOTE: BEYOND TOXIC

It was a "stop the press" moment. Hours before this book was printed, multiple allegations of sexual misconduct in entertainment, media, business, and political workplaces exploded into the public conversation. In the days that followed it was clear to us that we were witnessing a watershed event. Rather than one or two stories that spur handwringing and are then swept from the front page or disappear from the evening news, scores of stories poured out from multiple sources—many of them women in powerful positions who described being victims of sexual misconduct—from harassment to assault. The six types of toxic bosses we discuss in this book cause much grief and misery. But sexual misconduct is beyond toxic: it's unethical, immoral, and in some cases illegal. And, from the outset, was beyond the scope of this book.

When we started this project, the authors agreed to stay true to what we discovered from our toxic boss survey. The group that participated in our survey broke almost evenly between men (51%) and women (49%). Only one response was even close to describing sexual misconduct: "sexist." Why were bosses guilty of sexual misconduct left out? We aren't sure, but we have some theories. For one thing, if we conducted the same study now, people might be more willing to step forward with examples of sexual misconduct because the climate for discussion has opened. Second, it's possible that the survey participants interpreted sexual misconduct as fundamentally different from lousy management. Third, a survey like this one might not be the place one would reveal painful or personal information.

The six toxic types we discuss in this book don't include criminal acts. Assault, fraud, and other destructive acts create toxic environments, but the focus of this book, based on our survey, is limited to bad management and poor leadership. In terms of sexual misconduct against women, we direct our readers to www.ccl.org/womenleadership to review the substantial amount of work that the Center for Creative Leadership (CCL) has completed over the years pertaining to women in leadership. Some of that work appears in books, such as *Standing at the Crossroads: Next Steps for High-Achieving Women* and the forthcoming *Kick Some Glass*. Other work is reported in research reports and white papers. And a good deal of CCL's work about women in leadership drives our design of classroom experiences, such as the Women's Leadership Experience and the Technical Women's Leadership Journey.

We believe that #metoo and #timesup place organizations at a tipping point. While there is no vaccine against toxic leadership, powerful and far-reaching conversations about sexual misconduct—as well as increased scrutiny of organizations that protect the perpetrators—are redefining how we think of leadership and forcing organizations to take action. And for readers suffering under the thumbs of the toxic bosses we describe in this book, we hope that the strategies and tactics we provide help you survive your own toxic circumstances.

ACKNOWLEDGMENTS

Our thanks to the members of the Center for Creative Leadership's Leading Insights Community for their toxic boss stories. Thanks to Paula Morrow for managing the responses, to Jonathan Vehar for his ideas, to Kathy Schaftlein for her insights, and to Kris Downing for her suggestions. And special thanks to Harold Scharlatt, Mike Figliuolo, Donnie Horner, and Stevie Toepke for their insightful and valuable feedback on this book.

PREFACE

If you are standing in a bookstore flipping through this book or checking it out online, chances are you are in pain. If so, you already know what it's like to work for a toxic boss. You know they suck the air out of a room and the life out of their employees, and you don't need a research report to tell you that working for one is a nightmare. If this sounds like your current reality and you want help, this book is for you. Just know that it is not the kind of book that will mince words, make everyone happy, or jump-start the authors' status as leadership gurus. It is intended to be a practical, boots-on-the-ground guide to help you understand your situation and survive your toxic boss. So grab it and hunker down in the boss-proof bunker you built and get started. You can do this.

All three of the authors are toxic boss survivors. We lived to tell about it, but we lacked some critical survival knowledge and tactics that would have helped us immeasurably. In our work at the Center for Creative Leadership (CCL), we have met and worked with thousands of leaders and managers from around the world and from all kinds of companies, government organizations, nonprofits, and educational institutions. When the classes or training programs are done for the day, we often find ourselves sitting with the program participants somewhere having a drink. In this more relaxed setting and with the lubrication of 2.3 beers[1], the discussion leaves behind any in-class formality and the participants, male and female, young and old, will regularly share that they currently work for, or have previously worked for, an asshole. Our program participants are not whiners, and they don't fear challenges. Most are pros who have built a track record of success, and all of them have faced some degree of hardship over the course of their careers. And, for the most part, they have worked their way through the hardship by focusing on the issue, working harder, being flexible, and in the case of interpersonal conflict, working openly and honestly with the other person—to "work it out

....
1 The average drinking session, according to the American Nightlife Association, usually involves 2.3 drinks. Don't overthink this. It's an average. Nobody you know leaves two-thirds of a beer on the table.

together." But if you find yourself working for a truly toxic boss, none of that works. Toxicity isn't cured with carefully crafted feedback or through some kind of a win-win scenario where everyone comes out a better person. The bar conversations invariably ended up as a nightmare saga ending with a survival story. What people really want, we discovered, is a toxic boss survival guide.

The objective for any guide like this one, whether written for the business world, the military, worst-case scenarios, or even a zombie apocalypse, is to help you face your challenge realistically, identify the tools available to you, and deal with the problem. Our aim is to help you analyze your immediate situation, create a workable survival plan that fits your situation, and carry it out (including abandoning the situation, if that is what it takes to survive).

"Survival is the key word to remember—
not victory, not conquest, just survival."
—**Max Brooks,** *The Zombie Survival Guide*

The authors of this book have written numerous
scholarly articles, books, book chapters, and white
papers on the subject of leadership. And, if you are
unlucky enough to be under the dark shadow of a
toxic leader right now, none of that will help you—

unless maybe you decide to gather all of it together, pile it all up, and burn your way out.

Too many leadership books (including some of ours) tend to be too heavy on theory, too deep on the opinions and quotable quotes of leadership gurus and celebrity CEOs, too lengthy, and, ultimately, lacking in immediate, practical help. Our approach to this book? Keep it short, readable, and practical. There's a lot of research out there on the impact a toxic boss can have on people and organizations, but we have a feeling that you don't need a scientific study to tell you that you are miserable. Most of the research we reference is from CCL's Toxic Boss Project (see sidebar below) in which real people like you shared their toxic boss survival stories with us. Beyond that, we will reference research sparingly and only when we think it serves a purpose. We do reference movies, TV shows, and other lowbrow sources because we believe they offer more vivid and relatable examples than some leadership guru's latest book. And finally, working for a toxic boss is about as unfunny as you can get. We tried to bring a bit of humor to a subject that we all take seriously. Why? Because you will discover in

Chapter 5 just how important your sense of humor can be as one of your survival tools.

This book lays out a survival road map and is organized as follows. Chapter 1 describes the makeup of a toxic boss. What differentiates a toxic leader from someone who is just lousy, lazy, or is topping out according to the Peter Principle?[2] How do you know one when you see one? What are the warning signs? We will also discuss the predictable (but also sometimes unbelievably slow) process of derailment for these toxic leaders. Chapter 2 examines the detrimental impact toxic bosses have on people and organizations. How does working for a toxic boss cause stress and pain, and what is the impact on your brain, body, and soul if you don't have a survival plan? What happens to organizations who hire, tolerate, or even reward toxic behavior? These toxic bosses come in all shapes and sizes, and Chapter 3 identifies the six most common types of toxic bosses and describes the ways to tell them apart. Chapter 4 addresses the psychological aspect of survival. It draws from the research and practical evidence of people who

....
2 One of the contributors vigorously objects to this terminology.

have survived hardships, not just at work, but in a wide variety of survival situations—some of them life-threatening. We focus on the proof that one of the clear, consistent characteristics survivors have in common is the right mental attitude. Chapter 5 offers your template for a survival-based plan. Chapter 6 offers practical, straightforward tactics and action steps you can use right now to begin to deal with your own toxic situation.

THE CENTER FOR CREATIVE LEADERSHIP'S TOXIC BOSS PROJECT

Most of the examples and stories we use for the book come from people just like you. It is their perspective from the toxic trenches that provides the framework for the book. In May 2016, CCL invited 2,117 members of its Leading Insights Research Community to participate in an online survey on the subject of toxic bosses.

Members of the Leading Insights community share perspectives, participate in ongoing global research, and help us shape the future of leadership development. The community consists of global leaders who work in a variety of industries and roles. Members are from 65 countries, and approximately half are line managers and half are HR professionals. A total of 348 Leading Insights members responded to our survey to take part in the Toxic Boss Project. These respondents were 49% female and 51% male. 59% work for corporate/for-profit organizations, 11% in education, 10% in government, 14% in nonprofit, and 6% in other. 76% identified their region as the Americas, 11% Asia and Pacific, and 13% Europe, the Middle East, and Africa.

CHAPTER 1.

BEYOND INEPT, WHAT IS A TOXIC BOSS?

"I maintain it is much safer to be feared than loved, if you have to do without one of the two."
                                    —Niccolo Machiavelli[3]

CHERYL'S STORY

Cheryl, a senior engineer at a global pharmaceutical company, strolled down the hallway from one meeting to another on a day filled with meetings. She saw Frank, her group director, stomping toward her as if he were late for a flight. She immediately recognized his compressed-lip facial expression and started to step aside to get out of his way and try to become invisible. It didn't work. Frank beelined right for her, his neck and face flushed bright red, and he got right up in Cheryl's face. When he started talking, his voice was loud and right

....
3 Machiavelli. *Selected political writings* (Wootton, D., Ed. and Trans.). Indianapolis, IN: Hackett Publishing Company, Inc.

on the edge of being out of control. The verbal lashing started with a hot wave of the nastiest coffee breath she had ever endured at close range. "You really screwed up this time!" He was practically screaming. Before Cheryl could ask him what he was talking about, he blustered and trudged down the hall, establishing by default that his vitriolic attack was the last word on the subject. She felt like she had been sucker punched, and all of the half dozen people who watched the spectacle from their cubicles avoided making direct eye contact with her.

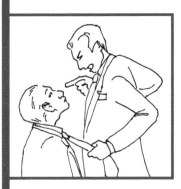

Cheryl was at her wit's end. She used to love her job, and for years she looked forward to coming in to her office every day. That was, until she got sucked into what her coworkers called "The Reign of Frankenstein." It wasn't the first time she had seen Frank go off, and it

wasn't even the first time she had been publicly humiliated by him. Embarrassed and angry that he confronted her like that in front of everyone, including someone she just hired who had only been on the job for a few days, Cheryl knew what would happen next. She would let herself cool off, and then she would approach Frank about the incident. He would act like it was no big deal. He would be reasonably pleasant—even charming—for a couple weeks and then, BAM! Frankenstein is back. This unpredictable hot-and-cold temper was only the start of Cheryl's problems. There was also the way Frank sucked up to the senior executives in their company and how he took credit for everything that Cheryl's team did. Cheryl had to admit to herself—she hated Frank.

The impact of Frank's behavior on Cheryl has been devastating. She can't turn her mind off at the end of the day. She has trouble falling asleep and has put on weight as she finds herself stress-eating. Worst of all, Cheryl really tried to work things out with Frank. She tried to take the high road and be the adult and the professional in dealing with his behavior

> *toward her and others, but to no avail. Frank is completely closed to hearing feedback and treated her worse for trying to talk with him about everything he has done. What Cheryl could not figure out is why none of the senior executives saw this. Frank sucked up to everyone above him in the company and just kept getting promoted no matter who he stepped on along the way. Although Cheryl had been happy at her company and her career was advancing, she decided that nothing was worth being this miserable and was considering leaving the company whether or not she found another job.*

What is a toxic boss? Chances are if you are working for one right now, you don't need a bunch of researchers to create a definition for you. For most of us, toxic bosses fit US Supreme Court Justice Potter Stewart's definition of pornography: you know it when you see it. And if you have spent much time at all in the corporate world, odds are that you have seen it (toxic bosses, that is).

Unfortunately, toxic bosses appear to be all too common. Often it seems that the only people who see the problem are the unhappy people who work for them. Toxic bosses cut a wide swath of pain and personal destruction as they pursue their ego-driven campaigns through their organizations. If you are unlucky enough to work for one, you don't need a definition—you need a plan—so you might want to skip directly to Chapter 5.

But what if you aren't sure if your boss really is toxic? What if you merely have a garden-variety bad boss? This is an important distinction since some of the survival techniques we suggest for dealing with a truly toxic boss are severe and are last-resort measures. It would be worthwhile to take a few minutes to make sure you are dealing with the real thing.

On the checklist that follows, put a check next to the behavioral traits that describe your boss. Only check the ones that your boss exhibits regularly and consistently.

❏ Overbearing ❏ Two-faced
❏ Impersonal ❏ Abusive
❏ Indecisive ❏ Micromanager

- ❑ Rude
- ❑ Careless
- ❑ Unreliable
- ❑ Obsessive
- ❑ Wimpy
- ❑ Critical
- ❑ Unavailable
- ❑ Annoying
- ❑ Incompetent
- ❑ Brown-noser
- ❑ Dimwitted

- ❑ Narcissistic
- ❑ Demanding
- ❑ Tyrannical
- ❑ Verbally abusive
- ❑ Insecure
- ❑ Belittling
- ❑ Egomaniac
- ❑ Unpredictable
- ❑ Bullying
- ❑ Amoral
- ❑ Arrogant

Now look at the number of boxes you checked in each column. The column on the right describes the attributes most commonly used to describe toxic bosses. The column on the left, while bad enough, usually just describes someone who is inept. While an unscientific measure, if most of your check marks are on the left side, you might just have a bad boss. That's not to say that working for an inept boss is a walk in the park, it's just that there are other tactics for dealing with a bad boss.

For example, bad bosses consistently demonstrate low self-awareness. Sometimes that element of cluelessness can be addressed by giving the boss feedback, or from the boss receiving coaching. Ricky Gervais, co-creator of the TV series *The Office*, said in a podcast interview that the entire show was built on one joke—that the boss, David Brent (in the original British version), has a gaping blind spot. He thinks he is effective but he isn't.[4] While none of us would seek to work for a boss like David Brent, we probably wouldn't consider him toxic—just clueless and inept.

On the other hand, if you checked off four or more of the descriptors on the right column, you may be dealing with a truly toxic boss. If that is the case, it changes everything. With toxic bosses, there is no feedback diplomatic enough to get through to them, and there is no win-win result to strive for because a toxic boss only understands his or her half of the win-win concept. Your goal at this point is not to help the toxic boss make the necessary behavioral changes so that everyone can be happier

. . . .

4 Pang, K. (2014, July 1). Ricky Gervais. *Typecast.* Podcast retrieved from http://typecastshow.com/

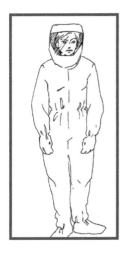

and more productive. This is a survival situation, and your self-preservation is your only priority. In this book, we hope to help you use your wits and any tools you have at hand to survive. With the right mindset, you can do this.

So what is a toxic leader? For the purpose of clarification, and because the world loves a definition, here is ours.

Toxic bosses are ones who use destructive, often intentional, behaviors to serve themselves and their own agenda, causing excessive harm to their subordinates and other coworkers.

Like any definition, it serves as a starting point. The bad news is that toxic bosses are not identical and can come in a variety of shapes and sizes. The one thing that toxic bosses have in common is that they spread their poison, killing the effectiveness and happiness of the people in their shadows.

CHAPTER 2.

THE DESTRUCTIVE IMPACT OF TOXIC BOSSES

"Rotten bosses don't get better. Any strategy
that assumes they can is doomed."
—Scott Adams, Creator of Dilbert

Miranda Priestly, Meryl Streep's character in *The Devil Wears Prada*,[5] may be fictitious, but there are plenty of true-life devilish bosses like her out there. The organizational and emotional wreckage these people leave in their wake is all too real.

THE PREVALENCE OF TOXIC BOSSES

Toxic bosses appear in many organizations and in all sectors—public, private, and nonprofit. Many of our clients have personally experienced toxic bosses and often have visceral and emotional reactions when relating their personal experiences. This begs the question: if toxic bosses have such

....
5 Finerman, W. (Producer), & Frankel, D. (Director). (2006). *The Devil Wears Prada.* United States: Fox 2000 Pictures.

 terrible effects on people in organizations, why are they so prevalent? Why do their organizations not see them for who they are and remove them from leadership positions for the good of the organization and its people? We believe part of the answer may be that toxic bosses are like a two-sided coin: they show the shiny side to their superiors who, in many cases, are unaware of the toxicity. To those unfortunate souls who work for them, they show the dark side of the same coin.[6] Toxic bosses can be masters at image control to the people above them. Toxic leaders don't contribute to healthy, thriving organizations but can somehow

....
6 In a former leadership role, one of the authors had a toxic supervisor working under him for years without detection. The most telling clues were continued poor results on annual employee climate surveys which persisted despite efforts to improve working conditions. But, without specific information, the cause was impossible to pinpoint. It took a series of sensing sessions conducted by the organization's Employee Assistance Program (EAP) to finally identify the cause and, even then, only when one brave employee spoke up during the final debrief. The suffering employees working under this supervisor had been cowed into silence.

produce results that their superiors prize without understanding the methods or the cost. These results are usually short-term and often last only as long as that person is in charge. In organizations that are focused on short-term outcomes, such as quarterly reports, without an eye toward the longer-term health of the organization, toxic bosses can thrive. Toxic bosses typically do not want to set their successor or the organization up for success after they are gone. Rather, due to their vanity, they would rather their successor and the organization founder in their wake just to prove how indispensable they were. They may also not

Years ago, one of the authors took command of an army unit from a toxic leader who was reputed to be the best leader in the organization. The outgoing commander advised him, "Treat them (the soldiers) like dogs. Never let up for a minute or they'll shit all over you."

The author was stunned upon receiving this "advice" and recalls thinking, "If that's what it takes to be successful, then I can't do it." Fortunately, he succeeded without having to resort to such tactics but only after going through a rocky transition period. He was nearly relieved of command due to a major incident as the unit adjusted to a less controlling and more empowering leadership style.

care so long as they get the next assignment or promotion they wanted, as self-interest is their primary motivation. The costs to the organization and the people in it can be immense, with the true cost becoming apparent only well after the damage has been done and often only after the toxic boss has left.

What is the impact of a toxic boss? Plenty, according to the results from our Toxic Boss Project research study. Toxic bosses incite low morale, fear, and anger in their organizations according to 96% of the respondents in our survey. Worse yet, the organizational climate itself becomes toxic and the negative mood is contagious. Some people respond to this noxious stew by leaving in frustration.

CHERYL'S STORY

After Frank's screaming fit and public humiliation of her, Cheryl is stunned. She is reminded of a quote from Machiavelli: "People should either be caressed or crushed. If you do them minor damage they will get their revenge; but if you cripple them there is nothing they can do."[7] *"Yup," she thinks, "he certainly crushed me!"*

With her heart pounding, she replays the scene over and over again in her mind, trying to decipher what he was talking about. She can see the angry look on his face as he screamed at her, and she feels her spirit crushed. She simply cannot go back to her desk and resume work right away. Not knowing what else to do, Cheryl escapes to the office of a trusted colleague and friend, Meg, who is a scientist, like Cheryl, but works in a different group.

Once safely behind closed doors, Cheryl unloads about Frank's latest verbal abuse, the complete unpredictability of his explosions, and the constant anxiety she feels as a result. Cheryl tells Meg that she can't get her mind off work at the end of the day, she's not sleeping well, and she is stress-eating, which has led to weight gain and further distress. Cheryl confides that she is angry and frustrated and sees no way out except to leave the company whether or not she

....
7 Machiavelli. *Selected political writings* (Wootton, D., Ed. and Trans.). Indianapolis, IN: Hackett Publishing Company, Inc.

> has another job offer. Meg tries to encourage her, but Cheryl has made up her mind to bail out *(intentional use of a survival term!).*

IMPACT ON RETENTION AND PRODUCTIVITY

In the Toxic Boss Project, 93% of respondents reported that they have witnessed some or a significant impact on staff turnover as a result of toxic bosses. Not surprisingly, toxic bosses drive out good talent. A high churn rate (attrition) is a clear indicator of a toxic boss in the ranks. Good executives and HR professionals know the hidden organizational costs of employee turnover. It can cost as much as $30,000 to $45,000 to replace an employee making $60,000![8]

High churn, or rapid turnover, also negatively impacts productivity. For example, not only is there lost productivity due to the vacancy, but the organization also has to manage the hiring and on-boarding process, which takes significant time and effort. Even once a person has been hired, there is typically a ramp-up process marked by less than

8 Kantor, J. (2016, February 11). *High turnover costs way more than you think.* Retrieved from http://www.huffingtonpost.com/julie-kantor/high-turnover-costs-way-more-than-you-think_b_9197238.html

optimal productivity until that person gets up to speed.

Those who remain when others bail out often hunker down in order to avoid being the next victim. Their will to expend more than the minimal effort is greatly diminished, resulting in lowered productivity (according to 87% of the Toxic Boss Project survey respondents). They also tend to use work time to vent and process their thoughts and emotions surrounding the toxic boss, as we see in Cheryl's case study. Teamwork and collaboration suffer, and gossip and rumors thrive. Lastly, toxic bosses often create more work as a way of dealing with their stress, not better work, which also detracts from productivity.

The toxins spread by these bosses also cause sickness to others. As a result of the oppressive behaviors of these leaders, 68% of the people in our Toxic Boss Project reported taking more sick days. In an example of the detrimental impact on a victim's health, a person said that one toxic boss "Has meetings to express anger for one to four hours and the staff was wore (sic) down mentally, they come out shaking, covering their face, will go home sick or almost brought to tears."[9]

IMPACT ON CREATIVITY

Toxic leadership crushes idea generation and risk-taking, which are the keys to a healthy and innovative organizational culture. People aren't creative and can't generate new ideas when they are in pain and "focused on organizational dysfunction."[10]

....

9 Staff (2014, January 28). Excerpts from military investigations into allegations of toxic leadership. *Washington Post.* Retrieved from https://www.washingtonpost.com/world/national-security/excerpts-from-military-investigations-into-allegations-of-toxic-leadership/2014/01/28/7b4610d8-886a-11e3-833c-33098f9e5267_story.html

10 Frost, P. J., & Robinson, S. (1999, July/August). The toxic handler: Organizational hero—and casualty. *Harvard Business Review.* Retrieved

General David Perkins, former Commanding General US Army Training and Doctrine Command, said, "...if you have toxic leadership, people will get sort of what we call the 'foxhole mentality.' They'll just hunker down and no one is taking what we call prudent risk."[11] In order to survive a toxic boss, many people will try to hide as best they can and wait until the person moves on to their next promotion. Needless to say, this is not a plan for success and innovation. Mark Zuckerberg, Facebook's founder and CEO, said, "The biggest risk is not taking any risk...In a world that is changing really quickly, the only strategy that is guaranteed to fail is not taking risks."[12] An organization in which no one is taking prudent risks is one that will fall behind the competition, and (paradoxically) risks irrelevance or even its very survival. In other words, not taking risks is risky, and toxic leaders, intentionally or not, suppress risk-taking!

---

from https://hbr.org/1999/07/the-toxic-handler-organizational-hero-and-casualty#

11 Zwerdling, D. (2014, January 6). *Army takes on its own toxic leaders.* Retrieved from http://www.npr.org/2014/01/06/259422776/army-takes-on-its-own-toxic-leaders

12 Fell, J. (2014, May 14). *As Mark Zuckerberg turns 30, his 10 best quotes as CEO.* Retrieved from https://www.entrepreneur.com/article/233890

DISILLUSIONMENT

On a personal level, the negative effects of a toxic boss are insidious. Like a chronic disease, the cumulative effects of the stress of trying to survive a toxic boss simply overwhelm most people. These victims become angry, bitter, and disillusioned. They lose faith in the organization for allowing the situation to persist. Many believe that senior leaders in the organization must know about the toxic boss and tacitly approve, so long as he or she produces results. But the psychological and emotional costs can be too much to bear. People report that their physical and mental health suffers. They lose confidence and begin to doubt their own abilities.

LOW MORALE...AND WORSE

Toxic leadership can do more than just make your life miserable; it can actually be deadly. In a story on toxic leaders in the army, National Public Radio reported that the Army hired an anthropologist to identify the factors contributing to almost 30 suicides or suicide attempts by soldiers in Iraq in 2010. The conclusions he drew as a result of the study were startling: in the cases he studied, the soldiers had significant personal problems but, in addition, they also had leaders who personally decided to "ride" perceived misfits hard, giving them the worst duties and intentionally making their lives miserable. The report states, "suicidal behavior can be triggered by...toxic command climate."[13]

TOXIC BOSSES: WORSE THAN COMBAT?

A badgered subordinate of a toxic military leader reported, "I was very glad to leave (organization name)...I definitely took the assignment in Iraq to get out of (organization name)...my blood pressure was high...it was just miserable..."[14] This person came to the conclusion that combat duty was preferable to continuing to work for the toxic boss!

---

13 Zwerdling, D. (2014, January 6). *Army takes on its own toxic leaders.* Retrieved July 20, 2016 from http://www.npr.org/2014/01/06/259422776/army-takes-on-its-own-toxic-leaders

14 Staff (2014, January 28). Excerpts from military investigations into allegations of toxic leadership. *Washington Post.* Retrieved from https://www.washingtonpost.com/world/national-security/excerpts-from-military-investigations-into-allegations-of-toxic-leadership/2014/01/28/7b4610d8-886a-11e3-833c-33098f9e5267_story.html

WHY DO ORGANIZATIONS TOLERATE
TOXIC BOSSES?

These toxic behaviors are the exact opposite of what our research indicates are effective leadership behaviors and what CCL teaches in its leadership programs. (If only toxic bosses could be like George Costanza in an old *Seinfeld* episode in which he decides to do the exact opposite of everything he would do normally and enjoys unprecedented success as a result.)[15] Toxic bosses are egocentric, insecure, need control, and have low emotional intelligence (EI), among other things. So why don't their bosses do something about it? Common reasons include:

- ✤ The toxic boss' behaviors can be hidden behind an outer shell of charisma. The boss has learned to play a part and is acting out a role as a charming person toward select

....

15 There is an episode of *Seinfeld* ("The Opposite," episode 86, [Season 5, episode 22] aired May 19, 1994) in which George Costanza (played by Jason Alexander) realizes that every decision he has ever made is wrong. Jerry (Seinfeld) encourages him and says, "If every instinct you have is wrong, then the opposite would have to be right." Thus, George decides that, whatever he thinks, he will do the exact opposite and enjoys unprecedented success as a result. If only our toxic bosses would do the same!

(usually higher-up) individuals. They "kiss up and kick down."[16] (This is typical of the "Two-Face" type.)

- ☮ Toxic bosses can be masters at image management—cleverly managing perceptions and manipulating the information that gets to their bosses. After all, they are much more concerned about their own boss's perceptions than those of the people who work under them, whom they tend to view as temporary.[17]

- ☮ They have a "toxic handler" who provides a buffer between the toxic boss and the unhappy employees, thus mitigating the impact of the toxic boss.[18]

Organizational Reasons:

- ☮ Senior leaders are sometimes clueless

....

16 D. Horner, personal communication, January 27, 2017.

17 K. Schaftlein, personal communication, July 22, 2016.

18 Frost, P. J., & Robinson, S. (1999, July/August). The toxic handler: Organizational hero—and casualty. *Harvard Business Review*. Retrieved from https://hbr.org/1999/07/the-toxic-handler-organizational-hero-and-casualty#

about what's happening below them. Toxic bosses are masters at saying what their bosses want to hear!

☹ Short-term results are often positive— "Frank hits his numbers."

☹ It takes great courage to deal with it, and employees would rather not start "turning over rocks to see what's underneath." This can be due to laziness, inertia, or simply maintaining the status quo. It's easier to turn a blind eye even though the toxic leader is causing lasting harm to the organization and the people in it.

Jean Lipman-Blumen, in her terrific book *The Allure of Toxic Leaders,* also makes a compelling case that these toxic leaders survive and thrive because they meet the psychological needs of their followers—particularly in uncertain or volatile times.[19]

In the extensive research CCL has conducted

....
19 Lipman-Blumen, Jean. (2005). *The allure of toxic leaders: Why we follow destructive bosses and corrupt politicians—and how we can survive them.* New York, NY: Oxford University Press.

on the phenomenon of executive derailment, we have observed that, in general, these toxic behaviors ultimately catch up to the toxic boss and cause his or her derailment and eventual downfall. The problem is that for many toxic bosses (and the people suffering under them), this process unwinds slowly—sometimes over the course of

a career. And, if you're anywhere near them when the implosion occurs, you might wind up as collateral damage if you're not careful!

"People leave managers, not companies."

—Victor Lipman[20]

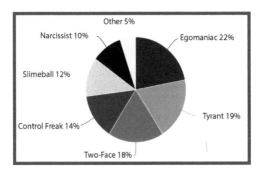

S potting a toxic boss isn't difficult, and based on the data we collected from respondents to CCL's Toxic Boss Project, they tend to group into frequently cited categories—what we call

20 Lipman, V. (2015, August 4). People leave managers, not companies. Retrieved from http://www.forbes.com/sites/victorlipman/2015/08/04/people-leave-managers-not-companies/#1021abfd16f3

Toxic Types. Providing a toxic taxonomy might not seem immediately helpful to you if you are hunkered down just trying to survive a toxic boss. But having an understanding of what makes these people tick informs the right tactics to use as we outline them in Chapter 6. It is important to note that most of the bosses did not have just one of these toxic qualities. More often, they displayed two or more of the behaviors described below. So, chances are, your toxic boss blends behaviors and characteristics—a real noxious mix.

The Egomaniac

The single most frequently mentioned toxic type was the Egomaniac. These bosses were consistently described as arrogant, selfish, and quick to claim credit for everything everyone else accomplished. The Egomaniac comes in many shapes, but one common trait was the degree to which they focused on building their personal empire at the expense of anyone or anything else. In our research, participants described the Egomaniac as "a shameless self-promoter," "a demoralizing credit gobbler," and "selfish, self-centered, and self-interested." The Egomaniac has some characteristics in common with another toxic type, the Narcissist, but they are not the same. Like the Narcissist, the Egomaniac sees himself or herself as the center of attention. The biggest difference is that the Narcissist is greatly influenced by the approval of other people, while the Egomaniac is not. In general, everything that the Egomaniac does is to satisfy himself or herself.

The Tyrant

History books are full of emperors, generalissimos, premiers, general secretaries, party chairmen, and supreme leaders. Therefore, it came as no surprise to us that dictators, despots, and other totalitarian bosses figured prominently in the stories from our study.  What sets the Tyrant apart from other toxic types is that Tyrants behave as if they are unconstrained by law, company policy, or virtually anything else. Tyrants control by oppression, often using whatever power they have in cruel and unfair ways.

One common way the Tyrant presents himself or herself in office settings is as a bully. And whether in the schoolyard or the workplace, bullies use intimidation to get their way. In the schoolyard, it was the threat of physical harm, and in the office, it is the threat of verbal, psychological, social, or vocational harm. A bullying tyrant can work solo, but frequently encourages others to gang up on victims and to rule by public humiliation. Survey respondents described their Tyrant bosses as "cutthroat," "demeaning," and "corporate terrorists."

The Two-Face

Many of our respondents described their toxic boss as two-faced. As a toxic boss, this phenomenon plays out in a variety of ways. The most common way is saying one thing to one person (or group) and then something completely different to another. "She portrayed a different face to superiors." "He was a triangulator who said one thing to one staff member and something else to another." Sometimes this is done to pit people or groups against each other. Other times it is to present the toxic bosses themselves in the best light to different people, particularly for the purpose of ingratiating themselves with superiors.

The other way the Two-Face spreads toxicity is by saying one thing and doing another. The immediate fallout from this is the lack of trust from coworkers from that point forward.

The Control Freak

There are some Control Freaks who, if they just have a mild case, might not qualify as toxic. They might just appear as anxious—a pain in the neck but not a threat to your sanity. A good example of this is the character Bill Lumbergh in the movie *Office Space*, hassling everyone about attaching a cover sheet to the TPS reports. In our study, the Control Freak was repeatedly referred to as a micromanager. Excessive micromanaging, combined with behaviors listed under the other Toxic Types, can create a lethal combination. The most common word used to describe what it was like working for the Control Freak? "Exhausting." However, there was no shortage of expressions to describe Control Freaks. "Domineering," "Unable to delegate," "Oppressive." One respondent said, "I had to overprepare for every conversation. It was a waste of my time." Another volunteered, "I always had to make an appointment to talk to her. I could never just drop in—and she was only two doors down."

The Slimeball

A total lack of integrity identifies the toxic boss known as the Slimeball. Untrustworthy and unethical were the words most often used to describe this individual. They break the rules to get out of bad situations or simply use dishonest means for their personal gains. The highest risk of working under the Slimeball is the possible damage to your own credibility by association with their sleazy actions. The Slimeball was described by participants as "Completely without principles," "Duplicitous," "A fraud," "Deceitful," and just plain dishonest.

The Narcissist

The term Narcissist gets widely used and is often misused to describe the Egomaniac. Why does it matter? The strategies for dealing with the Narcissist versus the Egomaniac are different, and

we will address that later in this book. Studies show that people who score high on measurements of narcissism frequently end up as group leaders. *Narcissists have a grandiose self-concept and see the world around them first and foremost as a reflection of themselves.* As a result, they have figured out how to use other people as instruments of gratification. They tend to be terrible listeners, are overly sensitive to criticism, and often have a complete lack of empathy for others. But perhaps what defines Narcissists the most and even trumps those other "qualities" is their relentless need to compete. To Narcissists, everything is a competition they must win, especially if it destroys competitors (real or perceived) in the process. The result is a toxic boss who can masterfully rally the troops in an "us versus them" battle cry, only to climb over the troops to position themselves in the rear. Narcissists might even ask you for feedback, but they don't want to hear it unless it is flattering to them or their ideas. Remember that Narcissists see their reflection in you, and if they don't like what they see, you become just another competitor— and eventual victim.

ADDITIONAL TYPES

Some respondents in the Toxic Boss Project used terms related to mental illness to describe their bosses. They described their bosses as bipolar, psychotic, sociopathic, neurotic, obsessive-compulsive, schizophrenic, passive-aggressive, and more. We decided to not create a separate category for this type because:

- The study participants were responding to behaviors they observed by labeling them with terms that require a clinical diagnosis. Any reference to mental illness should be treated with care and left to those with expertise in that area.

- Many study participants who used these clinical descriptors also used other descriptors so that we were able to classify their toxic bosses as other existing Toxic Types.

OTHER

Anytime you try to categorize human responses, they don't fit cleanly into nice, neat boxes. For example, one respondent, when asked to describe her toxic boss, simply replied "Steve." Those kinds of responses ended up in Other. So did any descriptors that comprised less than 2% of the whole.

INSECURITY, THE TIE THAT BINDS

The single most common descriptor that respondents used to describe their toxic bosses was "insecure." It didn't end up as one of the Seven Toxic Types because rather than standing alone as a category, respondents used it as an additional descriptor across all of the types. As a result, insecurity seems to be a common thread that ties most of the Toxic Types together. It is on this insecure foundation that many of the rest of these behaviors appear to emerge.

While this is not an exhaustive list, it sums up some of the common toxic types. The next chapter explores the impact of these toxic bosses on the people around them.

CHERYL'S STORY

As they continue their conversation, Meg helps Cheryl calm down from the initial shock of the surprise attack and asks her more about what Frank is like as a boss. Cheryl tells her, "That jerk's an unpredictable tyrant! He blows his top without warning and expects complete submission. And he's two-faced as well, telling us one thing and something completely different to Dave (Frank's boss). How does he get away with crap like that?! It's like he's above the law!"

Cheryl has been mentoring Meg, and they had discussed the possibility of Meg moving up into Cheryl's role when the time was right. But, based on what she has seen, Meg has decided to steer well clear of anything that has to do with Frank and the evil shadow he casts over his group. Meg isn't the only one. Word is out that if you want to work for an unpredictable jackass, work for Frank. And, even though everyone at their level and below knows that Frank is toxic, he somehow keeps his job.

CHAPTER 4.

THE PSYCHOLOGY OF SURVIVAL

"Energy and persistence conquer all things."
—Benjamin Franklin

B en knew what he was talking about. Not only did he survive a lightning strike, but he had to deal with John Adams, whom Franklin referred to as "Your Superfluous Excellency" and others called "His Rotundity." Was Adams a toxic leader? Quite possibly. Jerk-tastic? For sure. Either way, Franklin was onto something quite central to surviving, maybe even *thriving* in the midst of cringe-inducing toxic leadership. At the root of energy and persistence sits your mindset. Rest assured—we know from direct experience and from the Toxic Boss Project that keeping an energetic and persistent mindset is much easier said than done.

And yet… you can't change or control a toxic boss—that's just whacking the hornet's nest. What can you control? What do you have agency over? Where can you make the most difference? Your own mind, your attitude, and your energy.

When most of us think about survival situations, like being stranded on a desert island or lost in the woods, our minds often conjure up visions of survivors as lean and mean survival machines, physical specimens in top shape, or highly trained military professionals. As it turns out, decades

of research and case studies show that the physical aspects of survival run a *distant* second to the mental. The *psychology* of surviving is <u>the</u> X factor.

Reggie Bennett is president of the Mountain Shepherd Wilderness Survival School, and a graduate of, and a former instructor at, the world-renowned US Air Force Survival Instructor School (also known as "SERE" School for Survival, Evasion, Resistance, Escape). Air Force survival school is the ultimate test in endurance and survivability: globally deployed, airmen need to prepare for survival in any possible climate and terrain worldwide. Following his distinguished military service, Reggie has developed a reputation as a pioneer in bringing the key lessons of survival and related skills to the general public. Reggie can talk to you for countless engaging hours about evasion techniques, shelter building, fire-starting, the likelihood of Sasquatch existing (higher than you think), and the mouth feel of a banana slug. And yet, for all of his experience in the Air Force and teaching survival to diverse groups ranging from Special Forces and military cadets to women's groups and nonprofit agencies, one lesson comes through loud and clear, over and over: Positive Mental Attitude, or PMA.

PMA isn't about being a Pollyanna—that's not a realistic or helpful strategy when you show up to work for Emperor Commodus from *Gladiator* every day. PMA is about a reservoir of mental strength, an ability to reframe and focus, and a resilience defined by strength, purpose, and perspective. PMA (not physical prowess, specialized training, super intelligence, etc.) consistently emerges as the decisive factor in who survives and who doesn't at work and in the wilderness—and it is your primary antitoxin in the battle against a venomous boss.[21]

In the New York Times best seller, *Unbroken*, Laura Hillenbrand tells the harrowing real-life account of survival of Louis Zamperini (a 1936 Olympian) and his crewmates, whose B-24 bomber crashed in the South Pacific. Adrift on a tiny raft for 47 days without water or food and tormented by sharks and violent storms, one of the three crewmen, Mac, mentally gave up and died. "Though all three men faced the same hardship, their differing perceptions of it appeared to be shaping their fates...Mac's resignation seemed to paralyze him, and the less he participated in their efforts to survive, the more he slipped. Louie and Phil's (the other survivor) optimism, and Mac's hopelessness, were becoming self-fulfilling."[22] A classic and compelling case study of PMA.

The lessons from wilderness survival have

---

21 Speaking of venom, some estimates note that close to 50% of bites from poisonous snakes are "dry"—containing no venom. Sadly, the same numbers don't hold for the snake two offices down from you.

22 Hillenbrand, L. (2010). *Unbroken: A World War II story of survival, resilience, and redemption.* New York, NY: Random House.

remarkably relevant and helpful parallels with surviving a toxic boss. Building and tapping into PMA starts with three steps: recognizing, understanding, and accepting pressure.

RECOGNIZE PRESSURE

Self-awareness is foundational to effective leadership—and it becomes extra critical when dealing with your own personal tormentor every day. Chapter 2 highlights the perils of inhabiting a world of chronic stress. An additional peril is that many, many, many of us have grappled with the toxic situation for so long that our stress-filled edginess has become the new normal. And shouting out "Serenity now!"[23] won't bring back your better self. To get back to a better place mentally, you first need to recognize the stress and its impact on you—the heightened emotions, the slowed decision making, the increased lethargy, the withered engagement. Next, you need to recognize the various forms and sources of pressure. Once again, wilderness survival is powerfully (weirdly)

....

23 Koren, S. (Writer), & Ackerman, A. (Director). (1997). The serenity now [television series episode]. In *Seinfeld*. Beverly Hills, CA: Shapiro/West Productions.

relevant and instructive. The fascinating work on the psychological challenge of survival situations consistently boils down to several primary pressures that create stress. Take a look around you—then take a look at these:

The 7 Survival Pressures:

- Fear/Anxiety

- Pain

- Cold/Heat

- Thirst/Hunger/Fatigue

- Sleep

- Boredom

- Isolation

After reading this, your first reaction might be, "well, fine, but I'm not lost in the wilderness and am generally well fed and watered." But look more closely—the parallels between wilderness survival and coping with the pressures of a toxic boss in your workplace are *amazing* and instructive. When we (your author guides) were gutting it out through our own toxic boss events, we could easily check five of those boxes, and this framework really helps you label what's going on in order to then address it. Too stressed to be convinced? Let's make this painfully but usefully explicit.

1.   FEAR/ANXIETY

Think of the dread and worry that a toxic boss injects into your life and the environment. It gets even more uncanny when you chat with a survival expert like Reggie Bennett and he breaks the fear element of wilderness survival into these most common components:

⊛   **Fear of Being Alone**—Who wouldn't be afraid of being singled out, of being targeted by that Machiavellian backstabber, and as a result, having your colleagues avoid you and the giant bull's-eye on your back? We are social creatures with brains wired for inclusion and connection. An ever-growing body of research from across the brain sciences shows clearly and convincingly how chronic exclusion and solitary existence debilitates people, leaving them anxious, emotionally unregulated, unmotivated, *and* physically unhealthy as well.

- ✲ **Fear of Wild Animals**—Your toxic boss no doubt can come across as an untamed beast, and his or her impact on colleagues can similarly find them reverting to law of the jungle behavior.

- ✲ **Fear of Darkness**—No, your toxic boss doesn't make you fearful of the organization's electric bill going unpaid, but he or she very well might intentionally not invite you to key meetings, keep you out of the loop, hoard information, or even provide disinformation. Before you know it, you're in the dark about what's going on at work, which is disorienting and disengaging.

- ✲ **Fear of Suffering and Death**—This might sound overly dramatic, but it really isn't. Life in a toxic wasteland becomes extremely uncomfortable, awkward, and painful— of course you fear that. As for death, that toxic boss can absolutely contribute to the death of your career, the expiration of your path forward, the demise of your promising future, and an extinguished spark.

🕙 **Fear of Society/Ridicule**—A common theme in survivor stories is that survivors often have significant trepidation about being judged, criticized, or even mocked upon return. "How could he be so stupid to get into *that* situation?" "How could she have been so unprepared?" "Why would he make that stupid decision?" Who doesn't have similar thoughts and fears about our colleagues judging, analyzing, or even laughing at us and our inability to deal with Janice Janus or Mike Romanager?[24]

2. PAIN

Working for a toxic boss is exactly that—painful. The chronic stress, the unpredictability, the predictable discomfort, and the isolation are all extremely difficult to deal with. What's more, isolation has an intriguing connection to pain. From UCLA's Naomi Eisenberger and

....
24 Janus, as in two-faced, like the Roman god of the same name. As for Mike, well, read it carefully, à la Hugh Jass or Bea O'Problem. Highbrow, we know.

her fascinating "cyberball" experiment, we know that when subject to social isolation or exclusion, the same areas of the brain activate as when someone is undergoing physical pain. While you don't actually feel a physical pain sensation, your social and emotional brain interprets isolation as analogous to pain.[25]

3. COLD/HEAT

Toxic leaders work horrible wonders with temperature. One moment they warm up to you and you think perhaps you've turned a corner, and the next moment they've maxed out the thermostat and the heat is immediately on in the form of unreasonable demands and timelines and hot emotional outbursts. Or you suddenly find yourself on the receiving end of the cold shoulder; emails go unanswered, hallway greetings are icily distant. That sort of unpredictability debilitates your brain, your emotional equilibrium, and your overall ability to engage and perform.

25 Beilock, S. (2012, March 7). *Dealing with the pain of social exclusion*. Retrieved from https://www.psychologytoday.com/blog/choke/201203/dealing-the-pain-social-exclusion

4. THIRST/HUNGER/FATIGUE

As mentioned briefly in the previous chapter, chronic exposure to a toxic boss has a profound physical impact on well-being. In the most literal way, your toxic boss can wreak havoc with your eating habits—and your drinking habits, too. Slip on your metaphor hat for a moment, and you quickly recognize that perpetual toxicity at work makes you thirsty for information and inclusion, hungry for predictability and respect. As for fatigue, well, your efforts to just get by from day to day are downright exhausting.

5. SLEEP

Dealing with a toxic boss often massively disrupts our ability to enjoy regular, quality, restorative sleep, leading us to become even more exhausted. Just like a lost hiker in the deep woods, you can't sleep deeply if you can sleep at all, which only creates additional vulnerability to stress and pressure.[26] This

....
26 For a tactic-rich look at the impact of sleep on your leadership and performance, check out Connolly, C., Ruderman, M., & Leslie, J. B. (2014), *Sleep well, lead well: How better sleep can improve leadership, boost productivity, and spark innovation* [White Paper]. Retrieved from http://www.

is perhaps the most brutal and devastating "stress" or toll that a toxic leader exacts on us, since this stress so quickly and ruthlessly saps our ability to be our best self and to respond to the toxicity most effectively. A CCL white paper reports that "the sleeping brain helps the body's stress response switch off" and that "sleep deprivation limits the ability to respond to complex organizational challenges" (such as a toxic boss).[27] Seven to eight hours of quality sleep each night is essential to your cognitive and emotional well-being and to enhance your ability to deal with your toxic boss!

6. BOREDOM

On the surface, this seems like a bit of a misfit category. Sure, being stranded in the woods alone for days at a time can be life-threateningly perilous and not exactly a fun time at the beach. Yet, when you think about it, the stagnation that can come from life in the

---

ccl.org/wp-content/uploads/2015/04/SleepWell.pdf

27 Connolly, C., Ruderman, M. & Leslie, J. B. (2014). *Sleep well, lead well: How better sleep can improve leadership, boost productivity, and spark innovation* [White paper]. Retrieved from http://www.ccl.org/wp-content/uploads/2015/04/SleepWell.pdf

toxic zone, the lack of new assignments, or the back-breakingly mundane work that your boss piles on your desk can rapidly create a flood of ennui and disengagement. That boredom can quickly sap willpower and motivation, diminish self-care and resilience, and make you even more susceptible to the toxins polluting your work environment.

7.   ISOLATION

Closely related to the first survival stress, life as *persona non grata* is extremely stressful and diminishing—you feel alone while surrounded by people, and their perceived connection to each other only heightens your sensation of unwanted solitude. As inherently social creatures, we require some baseline of community and contact to live and perform at our peak. If your boss is a Machiavellian master manipulator, he or she can quickly engineer your isolation and cleverly disconnect you from your colleagues, which minimizes you in innumerable ways. Work suddenly becomes a lonely place despite all of the people, bereft of purpose (see "Boredom" above), and before you know it you're engaging in deep conversations with a volleyball about the true meaning of life.

Categorizing and naming the seven toxic boss survival pressures or triggers is critical—it then helps you with the next pivotal step.

UNDERSTAND PRESSURE

Stress is the brain's normal response to pressure. Leading stress experts like Nate Zinsser at West Point and Stanford's Kelly McGonigal remind us that our stress response is the brain prepping us to deal with some sort of external pressure, readying us to perform.[28] The adrenaline and cortisol rush, the accelerated heartbeat, the knotted stomach that you feel when your own toxic boss enters the room—all these feelings are entirely normal.

Dealing with the toxic challenge you face is twofold. First, as our own CCL stress master Nick Petrie explains, to really understand stress you first need to recognize the difference between pressure and stress. We often use these terms interchangeably, but they are distinct. Pressure is

28 McGonigal, K. (2015). *The upside of stress: Why stress is good for you, and how to get good at it.* New York, NY: Avery.

the external demand in the environment. We all face pressure in various aspects of our lives: deadlines, juggling multiple priorities, a significant other who binge-watches multiple episodes of *Breaking Bad* without waiting for you, surly teenagers, rush-hour traffic, or aging parents. For you, it's that toxic boss blustering or slinking around. It's super weird and pretty counterintuitive, but Petrie convincingly explains that none of those demands are inherently stressful; in other words, *stress doesn't reside in them*. Rather, stress is our internal response to that pressure, some of it biological and automatic, some of it created by our own tendencies to rehash and ruminate. Bottom line: the brooding narcissist on the third floor is not stressful; your reaction to him or her is.

Now Petrie brings the good news: "Once you understand stress is something you create, then you also start to see it is not inevitable. You can learn to work in extremely high-pressure situations and not feel stressed. In fact, you probably can recall times in your personal or professional life when you stayed calm and focused despite the high pressure of the situation."[29] In the next chapter, we'll talk more about your specific survival plan and how you'll embrace and overcome your own stress response.

ACCEPT PRESSURE

This step builds naturally from recognizing the seven pressures and understanding the stress they can generate if we aren't mindful and vigilant. To survive and even thrive in your toxic situation, you need to accept that some measure of stress is entirely normal—hardwired even—while simultaneously accepting that swimming in a sea of cortisol from day to day isn't okay. There's an illustrative scene in the very first episode of the hit TV series *Lost*, about a group of island-bound plane crash survivors. The scene in question isn't the mechanical-sounding monster, not the exploding airplane turbine, not Shannon screaming uncontrollably.[30] On the day of the crash, lead character Dr. Jack Shephard (more

....

29 Petrie, N. (2014). *Wake up: The surprising truth about what drives stress and how leaders build resilience* (p. 3) [White paper]. Retrieved from https://www.ccl.org/wp-content/uploads/2015/04/WakeUp.pdf

30 That, however, is a rather accurate version of how some people respond to an acute crisis moment—or to an ongoing toxic boss situation.

on his painfully obvious last name later), has a gash on his back that he can't reach. He convinces fellow survivor, Kate, to sew the wound up for him. To calm her overwhelming stress about it, Jack shares a story about a time when he was afraid, almost paralyzed by his stress response, but overcame it.

> *"Well, fear's sort of an odd thing. When I was in residency, my first solo procedure was a spinal surgery on a sixteen-year-old kid, a girl. And at the end, after thirteen hours, I was closing her up and I, I accidentally ripped her dural sac, shredded the base of the spine where all the nerves come together, membrane as thin as tissue. And so it ripped open and the nerves just spilled out of her like angel hair pasta, spinal fluid flowing out of her and I... and the terror was just so crazy. So real. And I knew I had to deal with it. So I just made a choice. I'd let the fear in, let it take over, let it do its thing, but only for five seconds, that's all I was going to give it. So I started to count: one, two, three, four, five. Then it was gone. I went back to work, sewed her up, and she was fine."*

Classic example (okay, a little too fluid-y even for us) of accepting stress, letting it in, and then moving forward with intention. This reminds us that surviving a toxic boss means avoiding the Scylla and Charybdis[31] of life-sucking "give-up-itis" on the one side and out-of-control anger and panic on the other. With fictional Dr. Jack Shephard's helpful prescription in mind, accepting stress is about reframing the situation, viewing the stress you're experiencing and the elevated levels of daily pressure as an opportunity, as what UC-Irvine's Salvatore Maddi has referred to as "the courage to grow from stress."[32] And guess what? That's really what this survival guide is all about—giving you courage and a real plan for surviving and even thriving no matter the size of the smoke monster or the Gorgon lurking in the c-suite. You always have agency, autonomy, and even responsibility for how you choose to respond to pressure, including the seemingly overwhelming and debilitating

....

31 A version of "between a rock and a hard place" from antiquity. Scylla and Charybdis were monsters on either side of a strait that a ship had to navigate between. Depicted in the super fun 1963 flick *Jason and the Argonauts* and also referenced in Sting's song "Wrapped Around Your Finger."

32 Maddi, S.R. (2006). "Hardiness: The courage to grow from stress." The Journal of Positive Psychology 1(3):160–168.

presence of a toxic boss. So count to five like Dr. Jack Shepherd, and we're on to Chapter 5: creating your survival plan.

CHERYL'S STORY

Meg gets Cheryl a cup of tea and Cheryl continues, "Meg, I don't know if I can take any more of this! I feel so angry, frustrated, and helpless!" Meg had been an athlete in college and had worked with a sports psychologist who taught her a lot about dealing with high-pressure situations. Meg suggests some mental techniques to Cheryl to help her deal with pressure, relieve stress, and develop a positive mental attitude. She explains that Cheryl's shaking hands, pounding heart, sweating palms, dry throat, etc., are symptoms of the "fight or flight" response, a normal stress reaction to a perceived threat. Knowing that Cheryl can't fight or run away (as much as she would like to do both), Meg advises her to balance those stressful episodes with quality recovery time. Cheryl's problem is that she continues to ruminate on those episodes, allowing them to invade even her off-work time. So, even when she's out of the office, she can't get away from it.

Over the next few weeks, after trying some of the stress management techniques that Meg had suggested, Cheryl feels better when she realizes finally she can't control Frank but she really does have say and sway over her attitude and effort. She is reminded of the old prayer for serenity she had learned as a kid.[33] Cheryl adopts a mantra, "I'm strong and have a positive mental attitude," which she writes several days a week in a journal and mentally repeats to herself throughout the day. She visualizes herself remaining calm and collected, no matter what Frank throws at her. She finds these mental techniques to be surprisingly effective at helping her regain a sense of control over her life.

Cheryl also starts taking walk breaks to get out of the office and clear her head. And she taps into the power of a support network in Meg and other trusted coworkers. She stops taking

---

33 *"God grant me the serenity to accept the things I cannot change, courage to change the things I can, and wisdom to know the difference."*

work home with her, makes a commitment to stop looking at laptops or smartphones at least an hour before bedtime, gets to bed earlier in order to get at least seven hours of sleep each night, and meditates before going to bed. And she starts to exercise again by walking in the evenings after dinner and on the weekends mixed in with a little jogging. These all do wonders for her sense of self-regard and inner calm.

CHAPTER 5.

CREATING YOUR SURVIVAL PLAN

"Survival doesn't have to be a suckfest."
—Reggie Bennett, Mountain Shepherd
Wilderness Survival School

Duct tape. Check.

Trash bag. Check.

Cotton balls and Vaseline[34]. Check.

Whistle. Check.

Not exactly a list of supplies that seems particularly helpful or suited to surviving your toxic boss? Well, if you're reading this by firelight in the awesome little hidden lean-to that you built from recycling bins in a far corner

---

34 Cottons balls dabbed in Vaseline are a fantastic tinder for fire starting. You'll impress your friends for sure on your next camping trip.

of your company's boiler room, it might seem quite apt. As it turns out, and as we explored in the previous chapter, the fundamentals of wilderness survival directly translate to surviving your toxic boss situation—you can draw from leading-edge survival tactics and action steps, adapt them, and apply them to your daily struggle with Attila the Hun. In an act of serendipitous symmetry, the seven stresses/pressures covered in Chapter 4 yield, you guessed it, seven Toxic Boss Survival Priorities.

An obvious point worth mentioning here— this is a *plan*. It involves thought, intention, and preparation—the opposite of stress-filled reactivity. This plan is not about guerilla activity or "elimination" approaches as depicted in *Horrible Bosses*. Your plan is about surviving the toxic situation as best you can until you can escape (yes, leaving is an option) or until external forces bring about resolution. And, as the opening quote to this chapter suggests, survival actually doesn't have to suck. If you consistently, intentionally implement most elements of this survival manual, you can make things better for yourself and others— and even grow from the effort and experience.

Seriously.

So, just as with wilderness survival, your Seven Toxic Boss Survival Priorities, in order of importance, are:

😊 Positive Mental Attitude (PMA)

➕ First Aid

🏠 Shelter

🔥 Fire Craft

🆘 Signaling

💧 Water

🍴 Food

Let's look at each of these in detail.

1. *Positive Mental Attitude (PMA)*

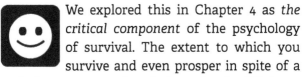 We explored this in Chapter 4 as *the critical component* of the psychology of survival. The extent to which you survive and even prosper in spite of a toxic boss starts and ends here. As the US Army Survival Manual states, "A key ingredient in any

survival situation is *the mental attitude of the individual(s) involved.*"[35] Your mindset is what you have the most control and agency over, and it will define the terms of your survival. The following two components of PMA are eerily consistent across survivor stories—build them intentionally into your strategy.

Laughter. Humor is critical even in the direst situations. The ability to laugh at oneself and even at the ridiculousness of one's precarious situation emerges consistently in wilderness survivor stories. You need to hone this ability in your toxic situation—it's a powerful antidote. If you spend time with soldiers, police, ER docs, and other first responders, you might remark upon and even be mildly shocked by their humor—usually dark humor. Don't mistake it for lack of empathy or concern—it's a key tactic in maintaining perspective, emotional equilibrium, and a positive attitude against the backdrop of some grim happenings. As Dwight D. Eisenhower—a man well versed in chaos and crisis as Supreme Allied

....
35 US Department of the Army. *FM 21-76 US army survival manual* (p.8). Author. Retrieved from https://archive.org/details/FM2176USARMYSUR-VIVALMANUAL

Commander during World War II and then as a two-term US president—commented, "A sense of **humor** is part of the art of **leadership**, of getting along with people, of getting things done." Be like Ike—laugh a little right alongside recognizing the gravity of the situation. If you stopped watching funny cat videos at work in order to read this book, fire up your browser! A recent survey conducted by Indiana University found that cat videos can boost a person's mood and energy[36]. Don't forget to include this handy fact in your next performance review.

Gratitude. Even when you have to report to His or Her Imperial Haughtiness each and every day, your life bubbles with blessings. Survivors talk about being thankful for the beautiful sky above them, the physical beauty of the landscape in which they were lost.[37] Maintaining an attitude of gratitude is how you become a survivor and

....

36 Not-so-guilty pleasure: Viewing cat videos boosts energy and positive emotions, IU study finds. (2015, June 16). Retrieved from http://news. indiana.edu/releases/iu/2015/06/internet-cat-video-research.shtml

37 See Laurence Gonzales' book *Deep Survival: Who Lives, Who Dies, and Why* (2017, W.W. Norton and Company) for more on the survivor's attitude, including gratitude.

a thriver instead of a victim. The research into the impact of gratitude has exploded in the past decade and shows consistent connections between grateful behavior and overall happiness and resilience. Keeping a gratitude journal in which a few days a week you document three good things that happened to you that day (preferably at work) and regularly writing short thank-you notes to people are simple actions with a disproportionately positive impact on you and your mood. Note: even in the midst of spine-tingling toxicity, there are three good things, however small. Every. Single. Day.

2. First Aid (for Others)

An extra challenging element of wilderness survival is injury—burns, cuts, scrapes, sprains, breaks, or concussions. In organizations dominated by a toxic leader, the same holds true. The mechanisms of injury can vary widely—demotions, insults, micromanagement, emotional abuse, etc. Your role as leader/survivor is first to take care of yourself as best as possible. Self-care isn't selfish—you do it to position yourself to provide critical first aid to "injured" colleagues. Just as you're instructed on every airline flight, put *your* air mask on first. Then, instead of reactively opting for "fight or flight," we can instead choose to "tend and befriend." This holds true for wilderness survival (Reggie Bennett's school isn't called Mountain Shepherd by accident....same goes for Jack's last name in *Lost*). Caring for and supporting coworkers wounded by your toxic leader provides a powerful purpose, gives an essential sense of meaning to the eight-hours-plus a day you spend at work, and builds a valuable support network. In some circles, this is referred to as "servant leadership," but whatever you call it, first aid for victims of toxic leadership enhances significantly your ability to survive and even grow despite the dire circumstance.

3. Shelter

 No matter where survivors find themselves, an early priority is to find or create some sort of protection from the elements. Heat, water, wind, cold— all can devastate PMA. Shelter also conveys a sense of safety from marauding beasties, snakes, spiders, and bugs. The same holds true for you and your lurking toxic leader. What is your form of shelter at work? You need a reliable safe place where you can go to reflect, recoup, and re-energize. Even Superman has his "fortress of solitude"—you're not made of steel, so you need one, too. And we're talking about a shelter *at work*—the respite that home often provides isn't enough and generally isn't accessible as needed during the work day. Maybe it's a conference room on a different floor, maybe it's the café around the corner, or maybe it's your favorite music coursing through a fantastic pair of noise-canceling headphones. It might also be your "alone time" when you meditate, go for a run, walk, hit the gym, or engage in other physical activity during the work day. Hobbies and avocations provide tremendously effective shelter, too, by giving us mental downtime and distraction often along with a tangible sense of accomplishment and control. You decide—but be intentional and *schedule* these activities into Outlook or your Google calendar just as you would a meeting or a phone call. Take a "toxic time-out." Have a space and go there *regularly*.

And, just like with first aid, as a leader shepherding other survivors, always consider the shelter you can provide to peers and followers also living under the boss's reign of terror—that "shelter" can be listening, transparency, a "walk and talk" around the block, or even a flexible schedule for some remote work time.

4. Fire Craft

In general, this is the part of wilderness survival classes that people get most fired up about (yep, bad pun intended). Learning actual fire craft sparks the inner pyro in all of us.[38] In an outdoors situation, fire is its own priority and it serves the others, especially PMA. Even in a wilderness survival class setting, it's remarkable to see the energy and whooping and hollering that happens when a

....

38 One of the authors was a scoutmaster years ago and has plenty of stories about having to constructively channel the designs of budding pyros. The best happened during the troop's annual pilgrimage to summer camp, when something caught his eye one day. He looked across the campsite to see a scout holding a length of burning nylon cord. Bright yellow drops of liquid fire fell to the ground making the sound, "*zzzip...zzzip...zzzip...*" The scoutmaster walked over to the scout, grabbed the burning cord, dunked it in a bucket of water then turned and left, all without saying a word. The scout never did it again.

group finally gets its fire started (quick tip: the old "teepee" approach isn't your best friend[39]).

In many ways, the leader's craft is fire craft. Purpose, connection to the mission, making a difference—all of those are the organizational equivalent of fire. Just as when camping, workplace versions of "fire" keep us warm and alert and draw us in and excite us. So, against the backdrop of a toxic leader who quite likely extinguishes flames, your survival entails keeping yourself and others alive and aware of the mission and meaning that continues to flicker at work. If this strikes you as a stretch, the data are voluminous on how important a sense of meaningful work, of contributing to something larger than ourselves, is to our joy and engagement—this "fire in the belly" or being "fired up" about work becomes exponentially more important as an element of survival during toxic times.

"Show the face your team needs to see."
—*Coach K*[40]

39 Do a Google search on "platform and brace fire" and never look back.

40 Krzyzewski, M., & Phillips, D. T. (2000). *Leading with the heart: Coach K's successful strategies for basketball, business, and life* (p. 157). New

Just as a good supply of oxygen is essential to keeping a fire going, your PMA is essential to keep the fire burning in the people around you. You must think and act with intention around how you can tend "the fire" and keep it burning strong and bright. During Ernest Shackleton's ill-fated Imperial Trans-Antarctic Expedition (1914–1917), against the backdrop of ship-shattering ice, fatally frigid conditions, zero communication with the outside world, and imminent starvation, he consistently and successfully buoyed his crew with his optimism and attitude—always tempered, but not brought low, by the bracing reality around him.[41]

Just as Harry Potter uses the magic Patronus charm to protect himself and Dudley from soul-sucking dementors in *Harry Potter and the Order of the Phoenix*, you can ward off the spirit-crushing toxicity your boss spreads by the bright light of your PMA and its connection to the fiery mission

---

York: Warner Books.

41 Alfred Lansing's account of Shackleton's voyage *Endurance* is a must-read. And yes, the name of his main ship was *Endurance*. Omen much?

that no toxic boss can extinguish.[42] (Yes, it's fair to compare your toxic boss to a dementor.)

5. Signaling

Any outdoors type will tell you right up front that a whistle and a signaling mirror are must-haves whenever you enter the wilderness, whether for a short, casual stroll or for a backcountry escape. Why? It's how you can effectively call for help; it's how you can help rescue teams rescue you. Unfortunately, and all too frequently, when we find ourselves trying to survive a toxic boss, we try to gut it out and go it alone. Likely due to some perceptions about strength or unexamined assumptions about what leader effectiveness looks like, we fall prey to a perilous limitation and fail to ask for help. In his marvelously subversive and entertaining volume *Orbiting the Giant Hairball*, Gordon MacKenzie relates a story about foolishly climbing down a cliff to access Blacks Beach in La Jolla, California. Ignoring the clearly posted

---

42 Barron, D., & Heyman, D. (Producers), & Yates, D. (Director). (2007). *Harry Potter and the Order of the Phoenix*. United States: Warner Brothers Pictures. You can find out what your Patronus is here: https://www.buzzfeed.com/ariellecalderon/whats-your-patronus

warning signs, he soon finds himself dangerously stuck and eventually in need of rescue—though he adamantly refuses to ask for it. Reflecting later that day (from the comfort of a bathtub) on his life-threatening episode, MacKenzie shares:

> *"I can only hope that the next time my incorrigible foolishness leads me into an immobilizing dead end, I will find the courage to call out for help. Ah! Courage, courage, courage. Courage to cross boundaries. Courage to admit idiocy. Courage to acknowledge impasse. Courage to open up to being rescued..."*[43]

Find that courage yourself. Like a lost hiker, send up a signal. Use that fire for smoke signals. Launch a flare. Ask for help from trusted colleagues, from an executive coach, from your church leader, from your boss's boss or from HR. It doesn't matter. What matters is recognizing that surviving your toxic boss isn't a solo activity. Asking for help isn't a sign of weakness at all—in fact, it's quite the opposite.

....
43 MacKenzie, G. (1996). *Orbiting the giant hairball: A corporate fool's guide to surviving with grace* (p. 80). New York: NY: Viking.

> **Signaling: Who can you call on for help or support? A Checklist**
>
> ❏ Friends   ❏ Family
>
> ❏ Coworkers   ❏ Clergy
>
> ❏ Superiors   ❏ Therapist
>
> ❏ Human Resources   ❏ Employee Assistance
>   (HR)   Program (EAP)
>
> ❏ Your favorite barista   ❏ Your dog
>   or bartender
>
> ❏ Ben and Jerry

6. *Water* and 7. *Food*

 Like most people, we found ourselves quite surprised that these two priorities sit at the *bottom* of the survival list. In many survival school activities, the unschooled and unwashed greenhorns (like we were), usually grab the food and then the water from a pile of limited supplies. As it turns out though, most wilderness survival situations last no more than seventy-two hours, and while certainly context specific, most of us can go three days without water and three weeks without food.[44]

But your toxic survival situation isn't seventy-two hours. It probably isn't seventy-two days. It's more like seventy-two weeks or even seventy-two months. Within that context, both priorities take on added importance. For an organizational setting, we frame the "water and food" priorities in terms of the proper care and feeding of your most important resource: your brain. The pressure, stress, and distraction of a chronically toxic situation at work alters our nourishment habits in debilitating ways. As we saw with Cheryl, unhealthy eating, binge eating, and weight gain are all too predictable, and they compound the lethargy, poor decision making, compromised confidence, and diminished resilience already in play because of the toxins pulsing through the office. The allure of Cheetos and chips and ice cream is tough to resist when we're feeling sizzling heat at work—they aren't called comfort

----

44 Even though Bear Grylls makes his celebrity guests eat maggots and other disgusting things during their two-day treks, it's not necessary, except as a ratings ploy (their reactions are priceless!). Most people find this a relief because they'd just as soon not have to forage for plants and insects. If you do need to eat a bug, use the following specs: six legs or fewer, no bright colors, and bugs that try to run away. Bon appétit!

foods for nothing. But that comfort compromises cognitive firepower. Compromised brainpower means weakened attentional control, diminished emotional regulation, lessened willpower—simply put, less of your better brain and your best self when you need it most. If you were going for a long, hot cross-country drive, you wouldn't replace the engine coolant with soda and motor oil with coconut oil, would you? Then don't do it to yourself and your precision-tuned machinery—your brain.

So, while they're still lower on the list, make health and nutrition a priority. Maintain energy levels through smart and savvy snacking. Keep yourself hydrated. Minimize alcohol consumption (largely because it negatively impacts stress number five from the previous chapter: lack of sleep).[45] See our tasty tips for healthy eating on the next page to improve your health and resilience.

. . . .
45 For more specific guidelines, head over here: http://insights.ccl.org/ articles/white-papers/the-care-feeding-of-the-leaders-brain/ and download a copy of CCL's White Paper, "The Care and Feeding of the Leader's Brain"

TASTY TIPS ON HEALTHY SURVIVAL EATING

CCL's Sharon McDowell-Larsen, a former professional mountain biker, triathlete, and exercise physiologist with the US Olympic Committee, recommends healthy eating in order to help you think more clearly and maintain long-term brain health. For both short-term survival and longer-term high performance, she recommends avoiding processed foods, meat, and cheese. Sharon recommends eating more of the following:[46]

- Leafy greens: kale, arugula, spinach, romaine and other lettuces, collards, mustard greens
- All vegetables, but especially cabbage (red and green), broccoli, bok choy, brussels sprouts, radishes
- Mushrooms: porcini, portabella, button, etc.
- Sweet potatoes and yams
- Legumes: lentils, black beans, red beans, chickpeas, pinto beans, edamame
- Fruits: blueberries, raspberries, cherries, acai berries, strawberries, grapes
- Seeds: sesame, chia, flax (or linseed), sunflower
- Walnuts
- Whole grains: oatmeal, quinoa, barley, brown or red rice, bulgur wheat, whole wheat pasta

....

46 McDowell-Larsen, S. (June 2012). The care and feeding of the leader's brain (pp. 7–16) [White paper]. Retrieved from https://media.ccl.org/wp-content/uploads/2015/04/CareFeedingLeadersBrain.pdf

Okay, we've helped you start to shape your plan. As it turns out, embracing and taking action on the plan is even more relevant because trying to survive is what most people do in toxic boss situations.

CHERYL'S STORY

Cheryl begins to focus on her survival plan. As she has always enjoyed the outdoors, she read a wilderness survival manual outlining the seven steps of survival and decides to adapt these to her situation. Now, thanks to Meg's advice, Cheryl attempts to adopt a PMA and finds that she can sometimes laugh at the absurdity of Frank and her situation. She also makes a habit of keeping a "gratitude journal" in which she daily writes down the things for which she is grateful. Both tactics help her feel more grounded and in control of her situation despite "Mr. Nasty's" worst.

Cheryl realizes that Paul, the new guy she had recently hired right out of college and who witnessed Frank's abuse in his first days in the office, is completely cowed. Whereas Frank is the terrible boss, Cheryl decides to provide spiritual first aid and strives to be the best boss she can be for Paul. She talks with him daily and finds out more about his goals and aspirations and what motivates him. Cheryl encourages Paul to take the GRE and apply to grad school so he can gain valuable credentials, which will lead to a pay raise and promotion. She also tells him about the company's tuition reimbursement policy, which will help fund his advanced degree. Like a plant that is watered after a drought, Paul shows signs of flourishing under Cheryl's care.

Cheryl finds her personal shelter by going to the company gym several times a week at lunch. She does yoga, walks or runs on the treadmill, and does circuit training in classes sponsored by the company's wellness program. She also does deep breathing and relaxation techniques daily. This becomes her personal recharge time, which gives her strength to bear up under Frank's toxicity.

In an effort to light a fire for those around her who are suffering, Cheryl thinks of what she can do to alleviate their condition. She knows that others look to her for leadership and does everything possible to instill a spirit of hope in the folks around her. She is careful to exude confidence and positivity. She also helps those around her regain their footing by reminding them of the company's mission, vision, and values and of the important work they do. Cheryl also regularly sings their praises to Frank and higher-ups in the company.

Cheryl signals for help by contacting the Employee Assistance Program (EAP) at her work. The kind folks in EAP treat her with respect and provide a much-needed outlet and offer counseling. This does wonders for her spirit, and she encourages others in her group to take advantage of this underutilized resource.

Finally, for water and food, Cheryl buys a water bottle for use at work from which she drinks two liters of water each day.[47] She cuts back on alcohol consumption, as previously she hadn't been sleeping well because the alcohol

---

47 Mayo Clinic Staff (2017, September 6). Water: How much should you drink every day? Retrieved from http://www.mayoclinic.org/healthy-life-style/nutrition-and-healthy-eating/in-depth/water/art-20044256

interrupted her REM sleep, causing her to feel tired upon waking.[48] *Cheryl also starts eating healthier, moving away from processed foods and adding more plant-based foods to her diet. These simple changes make her feel better, and she notices the weight she had gained through stress eating begins to shed away.*

....
48 Holohan, M. (2015, January 16). Beyond bed spins: Now we know why boozy snoozing is bad for slumber. Retrieved from http://www.today.com/health/now-we-know-why-boozy-snoozing-bad-slumber-1D80432196

"Survive and advance."

—Jim Valvano

I f you have worked your way through this survival guide in sequence, you have read about some common toxic types, been introduced to the critical necessity of taking an open and honest look at your mental attitude, and have started to create a plan. What remains is to break that plan down into specific tactics that will work best for your particular situation.

It might seem to you that you don't have a lot of options available to you—which is one of the things that makes working for a toxic boss so miserable. The reality is that you do have options, and who better to ask about surviving a toxic boss than those who have made it through to the other side? Participants in CCL's Toxic Boss Project described the many actions they took to survive working for their toxic bosses. The tactics they reported map directly to the US Air Force SERE School approach for pilots and others at risk of being stranded behind enemy lines due to aircraft downing and military operations—Survive, Evade, Resist, and Escape.

What works for you will, of course, depend on what kind of toxic boss you have and your specific context. When you view your situation with your toxic boss through the SERE lens, it gives you a framework for considering your options. Under each tactic, the actions are listed in the order of frequency mentioned by the respondents in the Toxic Boss Project. Suggestions for dealing with each of the Toxic Types can be found at the end of these four sections.

SURVIVE

This tactic sounds like we are stating the obvious. Aren't they all survival strategies, after all? Well, yes, but it means something specific in the SERE approach. This is

the tactic people use when they decide they are going to try to hang in there until the toxic boss issue resolves itself. Even though it is probably best used as a short-term solution, it is the tactic that people mentioned employing most frequently in the Toxic Boss Project survey. Is this the right tactic for you? That depends.

- ⊛ **Seek support with peers.** By far the most common action step in this category was connecting with peers who also have to deal with the toxic person. Sometimes just being able to talk with someone who knows the situation makes things just tolerable enough to survive. If you decide you will try to tough it out, this step can be invaluable. One participant mentioned that her coworkers would text each other an emoji wearing a gas mask when the toxic boss was on the prowl. Watch-out #1: Discretion is critical, as this could add fuel to the fire if discovered by your toxic boss. Watch-out #2: It can be important to share the honest hardships of your work with your spouse, partner, or other loved ones.

Just be careful that you don't allow your toxic boss to completely dominate both your work and your personal interactions with others.

⊛ **Focus on the work.** Most of us want a supportive work environment and a boss we respect and can learn from. Clean bathrooms and casual Fridays are icing on the cake. When that doesn't work out, and when the boss crushes the opportunity to make positive relationships, our survey participants reported that they gave up on almost everything except focusing on doing the best job they could. They focused on clients and other coworkers and didn't expect anything else from work. As a practical matter, this involves looking for your rewards, both extrinsic and intrinsic from places other than your boss.

⊛ **Hunker down and weather it.** If you think your toxic boss exposure is temporary and you can ride out the storm, then this might be the right approach. This is not a head-in-the-sand strategy. You are taking this temporary position as a way to survive. One participant described the imaginary retractable shield she constructed that deflected the toxic behaviors. She imagined the boss's insults bouncing off of her shield and landing harmlessly on the floor. The hunker-down step is a short-term approach, and the possible downside is that the toxic boss sticks around longer than you hoped. It was mentioned often as a preliminary step. Respondents reported starting here before they took a next, more drastic step.

⊛ **Stay honest to yourself.** Many of our respondents commented from a perspective of having worked for and survived a toxic boss in the past. Looking back, the one thing they were glad they did was to take the high road. They refused to lower themselves to the toxic behaviors being used by the boss, and when the dust settled, they were able to hold their heads high. Don't compromise your values. No matter what, at the end of the process, you want to be able to say you were the one who handled the situation professionally and like an adult. In *The Zombie Survival Guide*, Max Brooks reminds us that our main objective is to not become one of them (a zombie, not a boss).

⚙ **Pray/Meditate/Practice Yoga.** Finding a way to calm themselves and establish inner strength became a priority for toxic survivalists. Here again we are seeing the importance of PMA. Many people mentioned that the single thing they did that helped them survive was to practice yoga, pray, meditate, or work out. For some of our study participants, this was the key to their survival.

⚙ **Focus on your own career**. Similar to "Focus on the work" but with a longer-range strategic perspective. The difference is that focusing on your career involves taking a specific action that can position you for your next opportunity. Some participants mentioned that the simple act of updating their resume or LinkedIn profile made them feel better because they were doing something rather than just taking it.

- ☸ **Adapt to it.** This tactic was a bit of a last resort for people, but some reported that it helped them survive. Without going over to the dark side, they adapted to the toxic boss's needs. Feed the ego. Give up some control on simple tasks.

Is the Survive tactic the right one for you? It depends on what toxic type you are dealing with. The idea behind the Survive tactic is one of toughing it out. Each of the toxic types presents its own challenge to your endurance.

The Egomaniac	Just living with the Egomaniac is possible. Do not try to one-up him or her. Maintain your humility as much as possible. Remember that everything the Egomaniac does is to please himself or herself, so manage your expectations accordingly. Feed the ego in small doses, but try to not become a suck-up.

The Tyrant	How strong is your shield? Surviving the Tyrant is a question of how long you can take what many of our study participants described as abusive behaviors. This tactic tends to work best as a temporary strategy and setting a hypothetical end point with yourself is important. Then revisit your strategy to see if you can extend the survival period or if you need to try another tactic.
The Two-Face	Putting up with a Two-Face is probably more of a mindset shift on your part. Even though it adds work to your plate, maintain a paper trail to ensure you are clear on what you are told.
The Control Freak	Toughing out the Control Freak is easier said than done, since the Control Freak's nature is to micromanage everything that you do. One tactic is to judiciously and sparingly feed the control freak just enough to satisfy his or her need to be controlling *something* you are involved with.

| **The Slimeball** | As Max Brooks says in *The Zombie Survival Guide*, "The objective is to not be turned into one of them." Surviving the Slimeball involves putting up with his or her behaviors without playing his or her game. Beware of possible collateral sliming. |
| **The Narcissist** | One key to surviving the Narcissist is to not depend on him or her for any boost of your own self-esteem or worth. That feedback will only come to the degree that you support the Narcissist's image of his or her own superiority. Surviving the Narcissist requires a realistic understanding of your role as a mirror back to him or her of his or her positive traits. |

EVADE

This strategy focuses on ways to stay in the job but minimize the amount and kinds of contact you have with the boss.

- ☮ **Lie low.** Survey participants used the expression "Kept my head down" as much

as any other phrase. The difference between hunkering down and lying low is that the latter involves extra effort in avoiding the boss as much as possible by understanding his or her work routine. One participant said she figured out that she could tolerate her boss when she talked by phone and didn't have to be around him in person. On the old TV show *Cheers*, know-it-all Cliff Clavin described his "Buffalo Theory": it's the slowest and weakest members of the herd that are killed first. When you hunker down in the toxic office, you hope that the hunter passes you by and finds someone else.

⊛ **Ignore it.** A substantial number of people said they learned how to ignore the toxic behaviors. This might seem superhuman, but some participants mentioned "not taking the bait" as a successful strategy.

⊛ **Work from home.** Not everyone has this option, but why not ask? What is your organization's policy? One participant mentioned that working from home for just one day per week made enough of a difference to survive the toxic situation.

⊛ **Call in sick.** We don't recommend this because it isn't exactly honest, but a number of people mentioned this as an evasion tactic. And, as we learned in Chapter 2, toxic leaders can cause an increase in employee illness in their work environment. For some people, this step works for a while but, unless you can claim a long-term illness, it has a limited shelf life.

The Egomaniac	Avoiding the Egomaniac should help. Reduce whatever amount of contact time you can. The occasional ego-feed from you should help you avoid larger contact needs by the Egomaniac.

The Tyrant	You can reduce the impact of the Tyrant by avoiding him or her, especially during any predictable situations that you know cause the Tyrant stress. Some survey participants told us using the phone instead of holding face-to-face interactions provided a distance that helped.
The Two-Face	You may not gain much from avoiding the Two-Face. The Two-Face is still going to present one façade to higher-ups and another to you. You might be able to strengthen your network above you in the organization to reduce the impact of the Two-Face.

The Control Freak	Avoiding the Control Freak altogether is probably impossible—by definition. Even trying to create some kind of creative work schedule or arrangement might short-circuit the Control Freak's need to manage you. Negotiate your interactions in terms of workload. When the Control Freak adds to your workload, ask what he or she wants to take off your plate.
The Slimeball	The benefit of avoiding the Slimeball is that it reduces your odds of getting slimed yourself. Staying out of range decreases the odds of people seeing you as slimed by association. The downside of avoiding the Slimeball is that you might lose track of the slimy actions being taken and find yourself at an information disadvantage.

| **The Narcissist** | Of the toxic types, the Narcissist tends to be the most self-isolating. As a result, this might be an effective, if temporary, tactic to deal with this type of boss. Be aware that the Narcissist's need for adulation will require you to step in periodically to bolster his or her self-esteem, particularly during times of high stress. |

RESIST

This action step involves taking on the situation and fighting back. It is usually an all-or-none proposition, and the stakes are high. Win and the boss might be gone. Lose and you might go.

⊛ **Go over his or her head.** A surprising number of people went over their boss's head. Some went to the boss's boss, others went higher, to executive officers or even board members. This action did not always work, and when it didn't, it often made the participant's life worse—sometimes a lot worse. Many respondents described going to HR, with the majority reporting that they were disappointed in the results or a lack of action.

⊛ **Cover your ass.** The second most frequently mentioned action step was to quietly collect evidence of the toxic boss's wrongdoings. Participants mentioned doing this in order to cover themselves if things went bad, and also to use as evidence if asked by a superior.

⊛ **Give feedback.** If you work for a good boss, or even a garden-variety bad boss, this action step might work. You have to keep in mind that a truly toxic boss doesn't give a damn what kind of feedback you have for him or her. You may or may not be punished for bringing it forward, but the boss is definitely not going to change as a result. There is no win/win scenario that giving feedback will produce. Ask yourself what you have to gain before doing this. Many of the respondents did give feedback. The pattern seemed to be that they tried it once, and then when it didn't work, they had to take a different action step for themselves.

✤ **Stand up for yourself.** This action step might not work with most of the Toxic types we introduced in Chapter 2, but it just might work with the Tyrant. Think about it—in sixth grade when that giant kid with a five o'clock shadow picked on you, you weren't going to be able to talk him out of taking your lunch money or give him feedback about the impact his behaviors have on others. A bully is always going to be a bully, and because you can only avoid the bully for so long, standing up to him might be your only strategy. And, as bad as it is to say it, your goal is for the bully to realize he or she can't bully you and hope he or she moves on to bully someone else instead. A bully boss is the same way. Sometimes taking a stand is the right thing to do. Do it in private and calmly let the bully know that you don't care if he or she bullies other people, but you are not going to take it.

- ⊛ **Rally troops for a counterstrike.** This is high risk, but there could be safety in numbers. Plot an insurrection or a coup? Withhold information? Undermine via delay and inaction? Sabotage? Sometimes. If everyone is as fed up as you, this might work. In *The Allure of Toxic Leaders*, Jean Lipman-Blumen suggests that coalitions are critical for confronting toxic leaders. "When a single individual confronts the toxic leader as the representative of the unhappy multitudes, that individual is in danger of being ousted..."[49] It might work, and if you're desperate enough to engage in guerrilla warfare, we recommend you read the *Special Forces Guerilla Warfare Manual* for tips on how to "overthrow...a tyrannical government and establish...a

....
49 Lipman-Blumen, J. (2005). *The allure of toxic leaders: Why we follow destructive bosses and corrupt politicans—and how we can survive them* (p. 210). New York, NY: Oxford University Press.

just, democratic society." But, this could go wrong, badly wrong, so we do not advocate this approach (see the Bay of Pigs invasion, for example).

- ☺ **Manipulate him or her.** Some of our respondents said they play to the toxic boss's ego in order to manipulate him or her. The Achilles' heel of the Narcissist is an appeal to his or her vanity and pride, so this just may work. Others described making the boss look good so they could get what they wanted. Fight fire with fire.

- ☺ **Confront him or her.** A small number of people in the survey reported confronting the boss directly and alone. Some described doing this as a loss-of-control incident rather than something they planned.

Resisting and confronting any of the Toxic Types is a high-risk tactic. As Jean Lipman-Bluman notes, the element of surprise is critical, and you probably only get one shot at this. "Leaders who succeed in putting down the first attempt to unseat them quickly move up the learning curve.

By contrast, their defeated opponents usually withdraw in disarray, disband, or are eliminated."[50]

The Egomaniac	The Egomaniac sees himself or herself as the center of the universe, and any threat to unseat the Egomaniac's position is dangerous.
The Tyrant	Confrontation is a serious threat to the Tyrant. If you do confront him or her, expect the Tyrant to strike back quickly and severely. Expect your own performance to be called into question on the counterattack.
The Two-Face	Resistance against the Two-Face could work if the evidence is well documented and the confrontation involves both parties who are being played against each other.

50 Lipman-Blumen, J. (2005). *The allure of toxic leaders: Why we follow destructive bosses and corrupt politicians—and how we can survive them* (p. 212). New York, NY: Oxford University Press.

The Control Freak	Confronting the Control Freak could work if done tactfully. It probably won't lead to a dramatic difference in his or her behavior toward you, but you might be able to negotiate some rules relating to a specific area where you want to gain more control. It especially works well if you can help the Control Freak think it was his or her own idea.
The Slimeball	In our research, confronting the Slimeball usually meant reporting the person to HR. The more documentation and evidence you can produce, the greater the odds are of getting results. An unethical boss will likely respond to your accusations in an unethical manner, including false counteraccusations. Do not expect the Slimeball to accept the confrontation based on right and wrong. Do not attack this toxic type by taking a stand of righteous indignation. It is possible that you could end up worse off if this fails.

The Narcissist	If a Narcissist senses a threat, it can trigger a rage outburst. Any negative feedback is a threat to his or her self-image and, therefore, a threat to be eliminated.

ESCAPE

As we learned in Chapter 2, there is a significant amount of churn going on in organizations caused by toxic bosses.

- ☺ **Leave the organization.** Some tried to deal with it, some to make it better, and others said no more. Some planned their departure carefully, and others left without another job—they just couldn't put up with the boss any longer. This is permanent but may be necessary to spare yourself from further harm. The good news was that most of the people said that, in retrospect, it was the right move.

- ☺ **Leave your group or role.** Some participants managed a transfer to another position elsewhere in the organization. It works fine if you're among the first to try it. However, if you're not, it may be like trying to get aboard the last helicopter leaving the roof of the US Embassy in Saigon in 1975; you could find yourself out of luck.

⊛ **Take a leave of absence.** This is an act of desperation as it is only a temporary fix and, most importantly, it often means you take leave without pay. It could work if you think the toxic boss might implode during your absence and you can avoid the fallout. Or it might even give you a needed respite so you can recharge before you re-enter the toxic situation.

Escape is easier said than done. In our research, the majority of people reported that leaving was a last resort, and that many waited until they became ill, became depressed, or felt that their integrity or self-respect was at stake. Many reported feeling bad about leaving others behind. Yet, in retrospect, many of the respondents were clear that it was the right move to make and they are glad they did it.

CONCLUSION OF CHERYL'S STORY

Applying the stress-management techniques Meg taught her and focusing on her survival techniques, Cheryl feels better and is able to hunker down and ignore Frank as best she can.

A few months go by and Frank continues to be abusive and demoralize the staff. As much as Cheryl tries to rise above the situation, it is increasingly difficult to ignore. She finally makes up her mind to leave the company, polishes her resume, and starts job hunting in earnest. Cheryl gets traction and is invited in for interviews with several firms as she is a highly employable prospect. Cheryl soon finds herself being courted by two companies for second and third interviews.

Talking over a glass of wine one evening after work, knowing that Cheryl has decided to leave the company, Meg asks her to do something about Frank before she leaves. Cheryl agrees and decides to start with Dave, Frank's boss. She knows this will be delicate but asks Dave's assistant to arrange a private meeting.

When they meet, Dave greets her and asks, "What's up? Why the secrecy?" Cheryl replies, "I need to talk with you about Frank's abusive behavior. When he is unhappy with something, he yells at you in front of everyone without any specifics and without offering any suggestions for improvement. The morale in our group is terrible." After asking for more details, Dave sighs and says, "I've heard the rumors. But Frank gets results, and his group is one of the top performers in the company. Is it really that bad?" After further discussion and explanation, Dave looks at his watch and ends the meeting, saying he has another meeting to go to.

More than a month passes without any noticeable action on her complaint. Worse yet, Frank's abuse gets even worse than ever. "Is it due to reporting Frank to Dave?" she wonders. Cheryl tries a few times to schedule another meeting with Dave, but his assistant always says that he's busy and doesn't have time to meet. Frustrated by Dave's apparent brush-off and realizing that his nonanswer is his answer (i.e., he's not going to do anything), Cheryl decides she's had enough and goes to HR to file *a complaint. She tells herself that if HR can't or won't do something about Frank and the unbearable situation he has created, she will leave the company whether or not she has a firm offer in hand.*

Once at HR, Cheryl is welcomed into the office of Samantha ("Sam"), a senior HR business partner. Sam listens intently to Cheryl as she describes the entire situation, including Frank's tirades and her attempts to get Dave to do something, to no avail. Sam assures Cheryl that her report of abusive behavior will be kept confidential and that she will investigate the situation.

Over the next few weeks Sam investigates Cheryl's complaint, reviewing Frank's personnel file and performance reviews and discretely interviewing numerous people at various levels of the company to gain supporting evidence in order to triangulate Cheryl's report. What Sam finds is a consistent pattern of abusive behavior by Frank that has been allowed to fester for years. Although many lower-ranking employees knew of Frank's reputation, most senior leaders were unaware of Frank's dark side. And, the ones that were, including Dave, turned a blind eye because Frank could be counted on to produce strong results.

As Dave failed to address the issue after Cheryl reported it to him, Sam takes it to the executive team (ET) for resolution. After being presented with the evidence of Frank's toxic behaviors, on Sam's advice, the ET initiates a formal performance improvement plan with a 90-day probationary period. They also reprimand Dave for knowingly overlooking Frank's damaging behaviors. Frank's behavior improves noticeably, but the tensions persist and the group has been irreparably harmed.

Cheryl, who started her job hunt several months previously, accepts an offer for a group director position at a rival company. Several other employees in Frank's group, seeing Cheryl's example, also leave over the next few months. Finally, after a higher than normal amount of churn in his group, the ET terminates Frank's employment, but only after the human wreckage became impossible to overlook any longer.

ABOUT THE AUTHORS

The authors are all senior faculty members at the Center for Creative Leadership. Combined, they have worked with thousands of managers and leaders and have learned first-hand about the harmful impact that toxic bosses are having on the workforce.

Craig Chappelow manages CCL's 360-degree assessment line of business and has worked with client organizations in over 20 countries. He has published widely on leadership, including articles in *The Wall Street Journal, Harvard Business Review,* and *Fast Company.* A former biologist, Craig has held technical positions at National Starch and Chemical Company and Glidden Corporation and was a faculty member at Wake Forest University. He holds a bachelor's degree from MacMurray College and a master's from the University of Vermont.

Peter Ronayne has been working in leadership

development and executive education for almost 20 years, with an enduring focus on resilience and experiential learning. At CCL he manages several open enrollment programs and is a core member of CCL's neuro-leadership team. Pete previously served as a dean and faculty member at the Federal Executive Institute and has been a faculty member at The University of Virginia, American Military University, and Mary Baldwin University. He did his undergraduate work at Georgetown University and holds a PhD from the University of Virginia.

Bill Adams is a West Point graduate, former U.S. Army officer, and faculty member at West Point and Duke University. Since joining CCL he co-founded and serves as the faculty lead for CCL's government sector. Bill is an expert in leadership development, team building, and performance enhancement for all levels of organizations. He also has more than 11 years of experience in higher education teaching psychology, performance enhancement, and leadership. Bill holds a masters in applied-experimental psychology from Virginia Tech.

JOIN THE COMMUNITY

Thanks a lot for reading this book. If you made it this far you must already have mastered some survival skills for dealing with toxic bosses. We hope you picked up some practical tips from the book and a new helpful framework for thinking about and putting into action a plan to not just survive but to thrive. We'd appreciate it if you could find a fortress of solitude and take off your gas mask long enough to post feedback at Amazon. Remember, you aren't alone. The unfortunate reality is that there are enough toxic bosses out there to go around, and many organizations continue to put up with them. Since misery loves company, and since we have to laugh to keep from crying, consider hunkering down and checking out and contributing to the running toxic boss commentary from fellow survivors at www.toxicbosses.org/boss.

ABOUT CCL

The Center for Creative Leadership (CCL®) is a top-ranked global provider of leadership development. By leveraging the power of leadership to drive results that matter most to clients, CCL transforms individual leaders, teams, organizations, and society. Our array of cutting-edge solutions is steeped in extensive research and experience gained from working with hundreds of thousands of leaders at all levels. Ranked among the world's Top 5 providers of executive education by *Financial Times* and in the Top 10 by *Bloomberg BusinessWeek*, CCL has offices in Greensboro, NC; Colorado Springs, CO; San Diego, CA; Brussels, Belgium; Moscow, Russia; Addis Ababa, Ethiopia; Johannesburg, South Africa; Singapore; Gurgaon, India; and Shangai, China.

CPSIA information can be obtained
at www.ICGtesting.com
Printed in the USA
LVHW012143310720
662071LV00003B/146